Spotlight on Equine Nutrition Series

Joint Health
A Nutritional Perspective

Juliet M. Getty, Ph.D.

© 2013 Juliet M. Getty, Ph.D.
All Rights Reserved.

No part of this publication may be reproduced, stored in a retrieval system, or transmitted, in any form or by any means, electronic, mechanical, photocopying, recording or otherwise, without the written permission of the author.

Joint Health—A Nutritional Perspective was transcribed and expanded from a teleseminar presented by Dr. Juliet M. Getty. Transcription by Darlene J. Backer, CMT (DarleneJBacker@gmail.com).

Illustration, synovial joint, by Robin Peterson, DVM, FernWood Studio, Washington State (www.fernwoodstudio.com)

Book design, editing and publication preparation by Elizabeth Testa, Testa Creative Associates (www.TestaCreativeAssociates.com).

ISBN-13: 978-1490369051
ISBN-10: 1490369058

Printed in the United States of America

Preface & Disclaimer

Joint Health—A Nutritional Perspective is the updated and expanded transcript of a teleseminar on joint supplements given by Dr. Juliet M. Getty. The goals of offering the transcript in written form are, first, to make it a useful reference resource for anyone to use; second, to refresh the teleseminar participant's memory of materials covered.; and third, to offer the reader additional helpful materials on the subject. It is not necessary for the reader to have attended the teleseminar to get full value from the book.

At all times, Dr. Getty makes every effort to present the most accurate and helpful information based on her expertise and on the most reliable sources. She, her editor, transcriptionist and publisher take no responsibility for any results or damages that might be obtained from the reliance on the information and recommendations made in this book. We further take no responsibility for the inherent risks of activities involving horses, including equine behavior changes that might result in personal injury.

Advice about nutrition, especially in the case of illness, injury, disorders, or conditions requiring medical treatment, is not intended to take the place of proper veterinary care. It may be used in conjunction with such care to facilitate healing and maintain health. The information provided by Getty Equine Nutrition, LLC is presented for the purpose of educating horse owners. Suggested feeds, supplements, and procedures are administered voluntarily with the understanding that any adverse reaction is the responsibility of the owner. Furthermore, Getty Equine Nutrition, LLC cannot be held accountable for a horse's response, whether favorable or adverse, to nutritional intervention.

This is not a verbatim transcript. Obvious comments about technical matters relevant to the teleseminar process have been omitted, along with questions and answers off the specific topic at hand. Some text editing has been done to increase reading ease and text searchability.

Mention of a specific product or brand name is not intended to imply that other companies offer inferior products. Dr. Getty means no intention of trademark infringement by the omission of the ® or ™ designation; all product names mentioned are presumed trade-protected.

Juliet M. Getty, Ph.D. is an internationally respected writer and lecturer on equine nutrition. She is the Contributing Nutrition Editor for the *Horse Journal,* and her comprehensive reference book, **Feed Your Horse Like a Horse**, has educated countless horsemen and women in the science behind sound equine feeding practices. She hosts a monthly teleseminar series, one episode of which forms the basis for this adapted transcription. Her informative e-newsletter, *Forage for Thought*, is read by several thousand subscribers every month; she is also available for private consultations and speaking engagements.

The *Spotlight on Equine Nutrition Series* currently offers these titles (with more on the way):

    Aging Horse—Helping Him Grow Old with Dignity and in Health
    Easy Keeper—Making It Easy to Keep Him Healthy
    Joint Health—A Nutritional Perspective
    Laminitis—A Scientific and Realistic Approach
    Whole Foods & Alternative Feeds

Dr. Getty offers a generous serving of other equine nutrition knowledge at www.GettyEquineNutrition.com.

Joint Health
A Nutritional Perspective

Introduction

Joints, like all tissues in the body, rely on nutrients for maintenance and repair. If nutrients are in short supply, the vital organs (such as heart, lungs, liver, kidneys, and brain) have first access since the horse's priority is to stay alive. If nutrients are left over, tissues that are not life-supporting such as skin, hair, hooves, eyes, and joints will benefit. Therefore, the diet needs to provide all of the necessary components *in adequate quantity* to support the entire body.

Living, healthy, varied pasture provides a vast amount of nutrients and may be all that your horse requires to maintain basic health. It is the perfect whole food, leaving little else to provide except water and salt. However, the demands of work or performance, disease or aging can create additional requirements, which we'll discuss in detail later.

Getting back to grass...Once this living food is cut, dried, and stored as hay, it loses most of its vitamin content as well as its unsaturated fatty acids, which include omega 3s and 6s. This puts the horse at a nutritional deficit too large for the body to compensate for the damages brought by age or the challenges of hard work.

I talk about forage first because it is the very foundation of the horse's diet and must be flowing through the digestive tract at all times (For more on free choice feeding, see Appendix A). The stress of an empty stomach can lead to a variety of illnesses including ulcers, colic, and even laminitis. But it also causes oxidative stress—the formation of free radicals which go on a destructive rampage throughout the entire body, including your horse's joints, progressively damaging them.

Let's get more specific now. We'll look at joint supplements as well as specific nutrients that support joint tissues. We'll follow with your questions and my answers to address specific circumstances and concerns.

The Nutritional Foundation for Joint Health

Joint supplements

Athletes of all ages may benefit from a joint supplement. These products are designed to slow down the degeneration that comes with aging, replace what is worn out by excessive strain, and offer some degree of proactive protection against initial damage. But choosing one can be mind-boggling. The issue of joint supplements is vast—there are so many different ingredients and yet there is so little research on their effectiveness. Yes, studies have been done on whether glucosamine helps or whether chondroitin sulfate helps, and the answer is yes in both cases, and that's why we have them in the majority of joint supplements. In fact, the most common joint supplement ingredients are glucosamine (either in the sulfate or HCL version), chondroitin sulfate, MSM, and hyaluronic acid—these are what I consider the "go-to" basics for supplementation.

But there are many other available ingredients. Do they work? Yes, for some horses, and no, for others. Usually when I'm working with a client who has a horse with arthritis or some type of an injury, we start with those basics. If they don't help, we may up the supplement dosage a notch or we might switch to something completely different. It is often a trial and error process. It can be frustrating. So please expect that.

First, however, we also have to understand the nutritional foundation of joint health, and you don't read a lot about that in the scientific literature.

Joint Structure

We'll start with the make-up of synovial joints. The illustration[1] in the next page shows a synovial joint, one of three types of joints in the horse's body[2].

Spotlight on Equine Nutrition Series

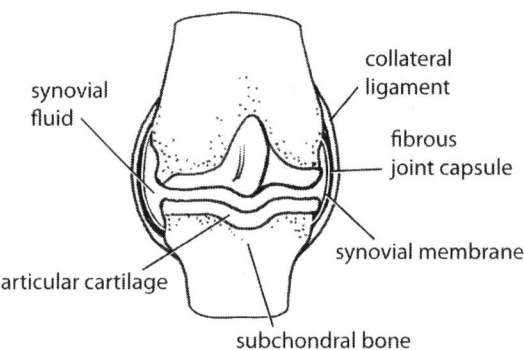

Cartilage cushions the surface of opposing bones. It is made of a protein called collagen. This very important protein is found throughout your horse's body. Not only part of cartilage, it is also part of tendons and ligaments. It is also a structural component of every blood vessel, as well as part of the skin—in fact it's what gives skin its elasticity.

Within the joint is a gelatinous substance called synovial fluid, which is encapsulated by the synovial membrane. Synovial fluid acts as a shock absorber to provide a frictionless surface between bones. And since cartilage doesn't have a blood supply, it depends on the nutrients in the synovial fluid for nourishment. Over time or with extensive use, this cartilage tends to degrade; it becomes thinner and thinner, and eventually it can result in bone rubbing against bone, which is very painful, of course.

We need to understand about cartilage so we can feed it properly and help it remain viable for a long time. The collagen portion of cartilage acts like a matrix or a latticework. Imagine a lattice structure that supports a plant like a climbing rose, and that's what collagen is like—it creates a criss-crossed structure onto which we can add things. We can add minerals and we can add protein sugar molecules called *proteoglycans*. Chondroitin sulfate and hyaluronic acid are a certain type of *proteoglycans* (*glycosaminoglycans* or GAGs) that attach themselves to the collagen matrix inside the cartilage, and they also exist in the synovial fluid that bathes the cartilage.

Collagen as a Tree

Another way to picture collagen is as a tree. In an article for *Horse-Journal*[3], Dr. Grant Miller describes cartilage that way. He continues the analogy to explain that when the tree—the collagen—breaks down through age and use, then everything attached to the tree (the proteoglycans) also breaks. And if the collagen is broken, the GAGs have nothing to attach to.

However, collagen breakdown is a degenerative, inflammatory *process*. So do we give joint supplements only to counteract inflammation, or do we give them to help slow down degeneration, or do we give them to feed the existing, remaining cartilage?

My answer is yes to all three of those reasons.

What we want is a strong, sturdy tree. We want to have plenty of collagen. Without it, there is nothing for the GAGs (in this case the chondroitin and the hyaluronic acid) to attach to. It's not an all-or-nothing proposition—the collagen doesn't disappear overnight; it's possible to remediate a situation and retard degeneration.

So how do we get healthy collagen? There are three nutrients that keep collagen healthy.

Quality protein

It's vital that there is quality protein in the diet, because collagen is a protein. By "quality protein," we don't mean green and leafy hay vs moldy and dusty (although that matters, too). We mean the degree to which the protein in the forage or other food can be utilized by the body. In order to be used by the body, proteins need the right "building blocks" (amino acids). Some amino acids are not produced by the body; these are called the *essential* amino acids—you can look at these as *essential* to be supplemented. So if your horse is on hay only, for example, and it's just one type of grass hay, generally speaking it won't be offering all of the amino acids that he needs, therefore it doesn't offer "quality protein." (And by the way, the crude protein measured by hay analysis[4] does not tell you the quality—the usability—of the protein.)

The solution is to mix foods. We need to make sure that the horse is getting several types of grass hay. Even better might be to add a legume such as alfalfa (or clover in the pasture). Legumes have a different amino acid makeup than grass, and so when fed together the two forages complement each other, giving the horse the amino acids that he needs to make collagen. Another legume is soybean meal, which is often added to commercially fortified feeds.

But mixing forages can have an equally powerful benefit, even without legumes. If your horse has access to a pasture that has a lot of trees and bushes and shrubs and maybe some berries or different varieties of foods, these also contribute to protein balance.

Wild horses don't suffer from a lot of joint problems because their diets are filled with variety; they eat all kinds of things, seeds and nuts and flowers and tree bark and leaves and so on, whereas domesticated horses tend to consume a steadier, more limited diet. You can simulate this variety to a degree by adding more ingredients—whole foods such as ground flaxseeds, chia seeds, split peas, pumpkin seeds, and ground or hulled hemp seeds.

Vitamin C

The second collagen builder is vitamin C. Vitamin C is absolutely necessary to make collagen—there is no way around that. Fortunately, your horse produces his own vitamin C, but as he gets older he doesn't produce as much of it. By the time he's in his twenties he is probably producing very little at all, so once your horse starts to get into his late teens I recommend adding vitamin C to his diet to help with collagen production.

Vitamin C has other roles, too. It's an anti-inflammatory, it's an antioxidant, and it's also a natural antihistamine, which can be helpful for respiratory problems and even skin allergies.

Copper and Manganese

The other nutrients we need to make collagen are the minerals copper and (to a lesser extent) manganese. These two minerals work together to produce collagen. Unfortunately, copper deficiencies can easily occur if the diet contains too much iron or too much zinc, which brings us to a discussion of mineral balancing.

Mineral Balancing

Zinc and iron both interfere with copper absorption so it is important to watch their ratios; manganese also needs to be in balance. Many joint supplements will contain copper. Some will contain zinc; some will contain manganese, and most will not contain iron.

Here are the desired numbers:

- Zinc and copper should be in a ratio of about 3:1, three times more zinc than copper. Zinc should not ever be more than five times the copper level.
- Iron to copper can be as high as about 5-7 times more iron than copper but no more than that.
- Manganese can be anywhere between 3-5 times the level of copper.

Now how do these calculations work? You have to look at everything you're feeding. You will add up the mineral amounts (not the percentages) that you are serving of every feed and calculate your ratios using the total of each mineral type.

Labels on commercially fortified feeds and commercial supplements provide the starting information. But because hay also has these minerals, it must also be included in the calculations. The best way to discover the contents of hay is to have it analyzed. The analysis should give the levels of iron, copper, zinc, and manganese plus the sugar and starch levels, which are also important.

Once you know your quantities, you do a little number crunching. The ratios will tell you whether you need to add some extra minerals. If so, I recommend looking for the individual minerals offered by HorseTech or Uckele. Use a gram scale to measure the exact amount. If you need assistance, I can help you with mineral balancing.

The stressed joint is inflamed!

Regardless of cause—use, injury or aging—joint stress results in inflammation. To counter this, the joint tries to regenerate damaged structures, including cartilage. Unfortunately, in most cases, *degeneration* is faster than *regeneration*, leading to exposed bone (and possible bone spurs).

Anti-inflammatory agents (GAGs such as hyaluronic acid and chondroitin) reduce inflammation by attaching to collagen to create cartilage. Therefore, the goal is not only to reduce inflammation, but to improve cartilage production at the same time. Supplementation with anti-inflammatory joint nutraceuticals have their place in joint care as well.

"First level" Nutraceuticals

Joint nutraceuticals to be tried first include:
- Glucosamine – extracted from shellfish or can be produced chemically through microbial grain fermentation. It is a precursor to GAGs.
- Chondroitin – comes from shark cartilage, cow trachea, or pig snouts. It inhibits enzymes that degrade cartilage, therefore may be more effective than glucosamine.
- MSM (methylsulfonylmethane) – mainly a source of sulfur which is needed for collagen production. Has a generalized anti-inflammatory effect throughout the body.

"Next level" nutraceuticals

To be tried if first level ingredients are not as effective as you'd like:
- Hyaluronic acid – a GAG, which is a key component of synovial fluid.
- Orthosilicic acid – organic form of the mineral silicon, which is found in joints and bones.
- Cetyl myristoleate – found in connective tissue.

Injectable joint treatments are often used instead of or in conjunction with oral supplements. These include Legend (hyaluronic acid), Adequan (polysulfated GAG), acetyl-d-glucosamine, and Pentosan.

Any of these may be useful for short term benefits, but in my opinion, it is far better to allow the horse to heal himself with the proper nutritional approach than to subject his system to repeated injections.

Whole foods and herbal treatments

One can enhance the overall nutritive value of the diet by feeding herbs and whole foods. Herbs also have medicinal qualities that may include pain reduction.

The following are worth considering:

- Potent anti-inflammatory herbs: *Boswellia*, ginger, grapeseed extract, rose hips, yucca, and *Perna canaliculus*.
- Curcumin[5], the active ingredient in the spice turmeric, has antioxidant properties, neutralizing free radicals and promoting healing.
- Omega 3 fatty acids from ground flaxseeds or chia seeds. Omega 3s reduce inflammation and should be present in the diet at a level that exceeds omega 6s. Grass naturally contains four times more omega 3s than 6s, and while some omega 6s are needed, too many can increase inflammation. Omega 6s are typically too high in most horse diets because the most commonly supplemented oil is soybean oil, which is very high in omega 6s. Flaxseeds and chia seeds offer 3 to 4 times more omega 3s than 6s. Feed <u>ground</u> flaxseed at a rate of ½ cup per 400 lbs of body weight. Do not feed whole flaxseeds. Grind flaxseeds yourself for each use (do not store) or feed a commercially stabilized product that has a small amount of calcium added to correct for the naturally high levels of phosphorus found in flax seeds.
- Vitamin C should be added to the diet, especially if the horse is past his late teens or if the diet consists mostly of hay. 3 to 10 mg per pound of body weight is appropriate.
- Quality protein should be provided by mixing protein sources.

Spotlight on Equine Nutrition Series

Don't rely solely on joint supplements

You can keep your horse's joints healthy by keeping him at a normal weight and providing a nutritionally balanced diet that contains the building blocks of collagen. Allowing him to move is a critical component to his overall joint health as well. The more turnout, the better. Standing for hours in one area will cause his muscles to atrophy (lose mass) and his joints will suffer. Strong muscles support and protect strong joints.

When a horse hurts, it diminishes his quality of life. Give him the nutrients to stay strong.

Let's move on now to listener questions.

---

[1] Illustration by Robin Peterson, DVM, FernWood Studio, Washington State. www.fernwoodstudio.com.

[2] Juliet M. Getty, Ph.D., Feed Your Horse Like a Horse, 2007. Chapter 15, "Joints, Hair, Hooves and Skin".

[3] Grant Miller, DVM, September 2011. Is Adequan or Legend Best? *Horse-Journal*, 18(9), 1-4.

[4] Not everybody has the luxury of being able get their hay analyzed, but you can have even a month's supply analyzed at a reasonable cost. You can go to Equi Analytical Labs. Their website is www.equi-analytical.com. I recommend the second test on their order form; it's called the Equi Tech.

[5] See Appendix B for more information about the benefits of curcumin/turmeric.

Questions and Answers

These start with the most general and move to the more specific[i].

Excessive iron in supplements and forage. Joyce comments that "most forages and supplements are too high in iron," and she asks if there is something to neutralize the iron.

> *Answer.* There's nothing that will *neutralize* iron, Joyce, but you can avoid supplementing it. And you're right to be mindful of this. Too much iron interferes with copper absorption, which can create a copper deficiency. Horses don't really need iron supplementation in the first place because they get plenty of it from their forage. For this reason, most actual joint supplements do not contain iron (or I haven't come across very many).
>
> For vitamins and minerals, there are some products available that do not contain iron. The one that I like a lot is called Glanzen 3 (HorseTech). HorseTech makes a custom product called Glanzen Complete and also Glanzen Lite Complete for overweight horses. It is a ground flaxseed based supplement with omega 3s, as well as the vitamins that hay is missing.

Carbohydrates and inflammation. Joyce asks if carbohydrates (either water-soluble or ethanol-soluble) have any effect on inflammation.

> *Answer.* Yes! WSC stands for water-soluble carbohydrates. These are simple sugars and fructan levels in your hay. ESC stands for ethanol-soluble carbohydrates and they're simple sugars. <u>Both WSC and ESC can raise insulin levels.</u> Whether it be the sugar and starch in your hay, or the sugar and starch in your feed, or starch from a cereal grain such as oats or corn, these all raise insulin levels and <u>insulin increases inflammation throughout the body.</u>

Usually our main concern is inflammation in the feet leading to laminitis, but increased insulin can also inflame any part of the body—including the joints.

Side effects of adding glucosamine and chondroitin. Joyce asks if there are side effects, and if so, what they are.

Answer. I have not come across any studies saying there are long-term side effects of adding glucosamine and chondroitin to the horse's diet. If a reader wants me to look at any reputable study, I'll be happy to.

Glucosamine absorption. Joyce asks about glucosamine not being absorbable.

Answer. Some people may be concerned about glucosamine sulfate versus glucosamine HCL. This is really a non-issue. Glucosamine sulfate has been shown to be more bio-available, or better absorbed, than the HCL version but the difference is truly negligible. Glucosamine sulfate is more expensive, it's not as concentrated in glucosamine as the HCL version, and it's more bitter, so that's why joint supplements will contain usually the HCL version. I have no problem with that.

Supplementing the horse that has Cushing's disease. Cindy L. has a 20-year-old Peruvian mare that has Cushing's, and she wants to know if there are any joint supplements for her horse's condition, and, if so, how much could her horse tolerate.

Answer. Cushing's disease secondarily ends up with insulin resistance, so cushingoid horses have varying degrees of insulin resistance, which means a horse with this condition needs to be fed a low-starch, low-sugar diet. Laminitis is a special concern in the cushingoid horse. In this situation, you want to avoid supplements that contain glucosamine.

Glucosamine may increase insulin levels in horses. We don't have enough research to confirm this in horses; however, we do have human studies that show that while it doesn't actually contribute glucose to the bloodstream, glucosamine tricks the body into thinking that the cells already have enough glucose. This prevents the glucose that's in the diet from entering the cells, and so it remains in the bloodstream; when glucose gets high in the bloodstream, the pancreas responds by releasing insulin. Elevated insulin levels can lead to laminitis.

So…although some insulin-resistant horses do fine on glucosamine, if you have a really tough case, especially if your horse is overweight or has had laminitis in the past, I would get a little more aggressive and not add glucosamine.

For horses that cannot tolerate glucosamine, I recommend Flex IR (Foxden Equine) which is a product designed for the insulin resistant horse. Not only does it have all of the relevant minerals, it has a number of other beneficial ingredients, too. It has a fair amount of chondroitin sulfate; it has 200 mg of hyaluronic acid, and it has some anti-inflammatory ingredients such as muscadine. It also contains a bioavailable form of silica, which is a mineral that is very helpful for joint and bone health, and finally, it has n-acetyl carnitine, which has been shown to help reduce pain. So, I like Flex IR.

Hock injections. Julia's 21-year-old Arab mare has some pain in her hocks. The mare has suffered some other health problems relating to an immune deficiency, but is now better. Julia has been giving her a joint supplement called HylaSport. She is thinking about the next step, which would be to do a systemic treatment such as Adequan or Legend. She asks if this is the right decision?

Answer. Adequan is a GAG (glycosaminoglycan) and you have to give a loading dose of it, then work it down to a dose once a month. It is injected either directly into the joint or it can be injected into the muscle. It has been shown to be safe and it has been shown to be effective. However, injecting things directly into the joint can, over time, cause more inflammation and the joints can swell—that aspect I don't like.

Legend is another injectable. This one is hyaluronic acid (HA), which is also a GAG and it can be directly injected into the joint tissue or it can be done IV, which is a little risky to do on your own unless you are competent at doing that. It does tend to work more quickly given IV. Legend can be given over the long term.

We see good results with both of these; they are, however, expensive and not all horses do well on them. I would try the HA for about three months and see if it's working well; if not you may want to rely on an oral supplement.

But here is a comment for everyone. Absolutely the first step, before you consider giving a joint supplement, before you consider doing injections, is to take a look at your horse's diet. As I mentioned, we want to make sure that the collagen is being produced adequately through high-quality protein, vitamin C and copper and manganese, in balance with iron and zinc. You also want to make sure that the horse is getting anti-inflammatory agents, especially omega 3 fatty acids which actually reduce inflammation.

Remember, on the other hand, that omega 6s *increase* inflammation. They're found in large concentrations in corn oil and in soybean oil, which is often listed as vegetable oil. I do not recommend them because of the fact that they increase inflammation. Wheat germ oil also has a lot of omega 6s.

The best omega 3:omega 6 ratio is about 4:1. A good source of omega 3 fatty acids is ground flaxseed, which has that ratio and which I recommend feeding at a rate of about one-half cup per 400 pounds of body weight. Chia seeds are another nice way to add omega 3s. Either of these would provide a good anti-inflammatory regimen.

For the horse in hard work or training where the joints are in heavy use, you might want to also consider adding some fish oils. Normally I don't recommend adding these because they're just not necessary in the basic diet (and horses don't eat fish!), but fish oils have been studied in horses and found to be beneficial to some extent. I like using them in extreme cases.

On my website, I offer a product called Kauffman's Omega-3F; this provides flax, also some fenugreek, plus DHA and EPA fish oils. This would be appropriate for more dramatic situations.

Again, keep diet in mind before going to a joint supplement. The nutritional foundation has to be there—otherwise, adding a supplement to an unhealthy diet is just a Band-Aid and it's not going to make a whole lot of difference.

Cosequin ASU. Debbie has a 12-year-old quarter horse that formerly did reining. His hocks are very painful. She has had him on Cosequin ASU for about two or three months but is also considering injections. She wants to know if the supplement is a good product.

Answer. Again—and first—make sure the dietary foundation is solid, then add a supplement. Cosequin ASU (NutraMax) is a very nice preparation. It has the traditional glucosamine, MSM, hyaluronic acid and the chondroitin sulfate in good amounts. It also has manganese but no copper.

And it contains a new kid on the block; the ASU stands for *avocado/soybean unsaponifiables*. A recent study done at Colorado State University found that ASU did tend to lessen the progression of osteoarthritis; it did not decrease pain directly in the way that, for example, an anti-inflammatory such as MSM might. (MSM is actually a sulfur source and it's a natural anti-inflammatory; not specific to the joints, MSM will reduce inflammation anywhere in the body which is how it works to relieve pain.)

Debbie, if you've had good results with the Cosequin ASU, by all means continue using it. As I mentioned, finding the supplement that is effective for your horse's specific needs is a trial-and-error type of thing.

If you find that it's not doing the job that you need, then you can go to the injections. You could start with the Adequan and then you can move on to the Legend if you need to.

Some people choose to do glucosamine injections. Glucosamine is a precursor to GAGs. Adding glucosamine doesn't directly affect the synovial fluid; rather, it helps increase the GAGs in the synovial fluid, so sometimes that's very helpful and a lot less expensive than the other types of injections.

Combination Supplements & SmartFlex Senior. Cindy D. has been using a combination product called SmartFlex Senior (SmartPak) and asks if combination products are as effective as giving individual products.

Answer. According to the SmartPak website, SmartFlex Senior is designed to support older horses in the areas of joint health, digestive function, and antioxidants to protect the immune system. The product contains a variety of ingredients, but nothing with omega 3s.

Its probiotics and digestive enzymes will be helpful for the senior horse, as will its superoxide dismutase, which is an enzyme with antioxidant properties (though its bioavailability is questionable since it may be digested within the small intestine). It has adequate amounts of the anti-inflammatory MSM. It contains chondroitin sulfate, but only 500 mg; that might be adequate, but I prefer to see a little more than that. It contains only 50 mg of hyaluronic acid, which I prefer at 100 mg or more. It contains an herb called *Boswellia serrata*, which is a good anti-inflammatory. Devil's claw offers pain relief, but its use carries some caveats: One should never, never give devil's claw to a pregnant mare—it can produce abortions; and devil's claw is not the best idea for horses that are prone toward or (in the case of hard working or stressed horses) at risk for ulcers because it increases acid production in the stomach.

Combination products are not necessarily less effective, but as you can see, they can be less than complete, so you need to take the whole dietary picture into consideration—including vitamins and minerals, which in the case of Cosequin ASU, the product does not contain.

It is possible to find a more complete combination product, if you need to supplement vitamins and minerals. I prefer one called Exceed 6-Way (Med-Vet Pharmaceuticals). It's relatively new. It contains a nice joint supplementation but it also protects the hooves and the skin and digestion. It has herbs and probiotics that help with gut integrity, and it has a variety of vitamins and minerals. It is possible that this product would cover all your horse's needs for supplementation. Again, look at the whole diet, then make your choices to fill in any gaps.

Aging gracefully. Miriam is a hoof care professional and she has a client horse between 15 and 18 years of age with osteoarthritis in the pedal bone. She asks for a suggestion on the best type of supplementation to let him age gracefully with as little pain as possible.

Answer. First, considering the horse's age, give him 10,000 mg of vitamin C per day, plus ground flaxseed to provide omega 3 fatty acids. Do this for approximately three or four months and see if you notice an improvement. It does take time, so if the improvement is even slight, continue with it for another three or four months. I have found that many senior horses do fabulously well on just those two things, assuming that the diet also has the vitamins and minerals that he needs.

If a horse is on a lush, fresh, healthy pasture with a variety of grasses, then generally we don't need supplementation during the growing season. However in winter most horses are changed to only hay, which contains very few vitamins; it certainly doesn't contain any omega 3s. So it's very important to supplement those things.

You also want to make sure that the horse is getting some other source of hay like alfalfa to boost the protein quality in the diet (remember: to help with collagen production).

So do those things first. Then, if that's not helpful or you need extra support, add other elements in a progression. I would start with something simple—a good all-around joint supplement. Three I turn to often are Matrix 5 H/A (Med-Vet Pharmaceuticals), HylaSport CTS (HorseTech), and ActiFlex (Cox Veterinary Laboratory); each has its own appropriate applications.

Spotlight on Equine Nutrition Series

Matrix 5 H/A is a nice all-around joint supplement with adequate levels of the basics, including 125 mg of hyaluronic acid (HA). It has only enough vitamin C to improve the absorption of the glucosamine so don't rely on that for a primary vitamin C supplement—you'll need to add more for the aging horse. Matrix 5 H/A has the necessary zinc, copper and manganese, plus a little bit of vitamin E.

Another choice would be HylaSport CTS. You can take a look at it on my website or go to HorseTech's website. HylaSport CTS contains omega 3s, some type 2 collagen, and the anti-inflammatory action of grapeseed extract. It also includes some silica which is a mineral that does seem to be very helpful.

Finally, you could try ActiFlex; it comes in a liquid or the powder. Actiflex does contain glucosamine which may make the product inappropriate for an insulin-resistant horse, but I have had very good results with Actiflex for healthy horses needing more than a simple joint supplement. This one also has the *Perna canaliculus*, which is green-lipped mussel, kind of an odd thing to add to a joint supplement but it is high in GAGs and also omega 3s so that's a good choice as well.

I would try any of those three first, depending on the horse's specific needs. If those don't help, then we can build up to something else. Here are some suggestions:

Cetyl-Flex H/A (Med-Vet), which has cetyl myristoleate, helps some horses. It also contains hyaluronic acid.

KeraFlex EQ (Foxden) with hyaluronic acid is a relatively new product from Foxden Equine and it does not contain any glucosamine or chondroitin. In fact, it's not derived from any shellfish or shark cartilage; it's actually made from New Zealand wool, and it contains a proprietary ingredient called Cynatine FLX. There are not a lot of studies to refer to on this but it does seem to have significant anti-inflammatory properties; some of my clients use it successfully when other things haven't worked.

The other one that I often go to is simply a bioavailable silicon; it's called OrthoPur Si (HorseTech). This one is very effective for horses that don't respond well to basic glucosamine, MSM, chondroitin, and so on.

Herbal products. Miriam asks about two herb-based products, Sinew-X and Antiflam (both by Omega Alpha).

Answer. The Equine Sinew-X has glucosamine sulfate and MSM, plus some herbs that claim to be anti-inflammatory to relieve pain. The Antiflam is largely herbal with MSM. First of all, remember that herbs—as "natural" as they are—nevertheless contain drugs. I am not an herbalist, so I cannot tell you if the *Rehmannia glutinosa* or *Gentian macrophylla* in these products have long-term side effects. All medicinal herbs contain diluted forms of medications which could have side effects over time. They can also interact with other medications (and herbs) that your horse may be on, so I would look into those carefully. You can research them on your own if you like or consult with an herbalist.

Preventive measures to protect joints in young horses. Miriam has several young horses and ponies all under the age of six. She joins several others in asking about the wisdom of giving supplements to prevent damage as the youngsters train and age.

Answer. There are two schools of thought about this. Some people believe in supplementing young horses to prevent problems down the road, while others say it's not necessary. I tend to be in the second camp because if the young horse has a balanced, healthful diet—good quality protein and all the necessary vitamins and minerals in balance—then the horse will be able to produce adequate amounts of collagen and have healthy cartilage and healthy synovial fluid to bathe and nourish that cartilage, so a joint supplement will not be necessary. However, MAYBE IF the youngster is working a great deal and has an inordinate amount of stress and strain on the joints (in hard training in reining or cutting, for example), then you may want to consider supplementing chondroitin sulfate and/or hyaluronic acid (Su-Per Hyaluronic Acid (Gateway)is one choice) to help suppress the enzymatic activity that destroys cartilage. The key word is MAYBE. You have to look closely at the horse's health, his work demands, and his diet in general, including your hay analysis. If at all possible, however, I prefer to not to supplement young horses.

Products: Recovery EQ (SmartPak) and Finish Line Fluid Action. Adele asks about these.

Answer. Recovery EQ has a listed ingredient called Nutricol, which is proprietary so I have no idea about its makeup. If it works well, then continue using it. I would say that the Finish Line Fluid Action, however, is inadequate: It doesn't have enough glucosamine, it has only 100 mg of MSM. I would go with the HylaSport CTS instead.

Hock clicking or popping. Adele asks if this is damage or air in the joint.

Answer. Without watching your horse move, my answer is qualified. However, in general, I wouldn't worry about that unless there is evidence of pain or swelling. The sound is usually air or sometimes it's caused by a degeneration as the horse ages, from a ligament that has loosened and lost some of its integrity. If you're concerned about the ligament integrity, then just make sure that the diet is balanced.

When is glucosamine not advised? Terry asks if there is a situation when a horse should not be on joint supplements, and if there are any foods that should be avoided with supplements.

Answer. As I've mentioned, glucosamine may be inappropriate for the insulin resistant horse. As for foods, there's nothing in joint supplements that interacts with them.

Long-term glucosamine use. Terry asks if supplementing with glucosamine will destroy the joints over a period of time.

Answer. Some time ago a study was published in *Lancet* that showed no long-term detrimental effects of glucosamine so I would not be concerned about that.

Flaxseed for easy keepers and/or insulin resistant horses. Terry asks if it's safe to feed flaxseed to easy keepers or insulin resistant horses.

Answer. Omega 3s, which flaxseed oil has in abundance, decrease insulin levels (increase good insulin sensitivity) so that it's very appropriate for an insulin-resistant horse. Flaxseed can actually help an overweight horse to burn fat—when you lower insulin levels, the body will allow fat to burn; when insulin is high, it will not.

Suspensory Saver (Figuerola Labs). Pamela asks about this product.

Answer. Suspensory Saver does contain some helpful ingredients but their product listing doesn't tell me the exact amount of any so I cannot speak to its balance or adequacy. It has n-acetyl carnitine, which helps the body derive energy during activity. It has bioflavonoids from herbs. It has MSM. It has Co Q-10, which is very worthwhile as a potent antioxidant. I can't tell you more than that.

Degenerative suspensory ligament desmitis (DSLD) and other ligament problems. Lynn's horse has been diagnosed with this debilitating disorder. She asks for supplementation and dietary advice.

Answer. DSLD is a genetic disorder, more recently called "equine systemic proteoglycan accumulation," in which proteoglycans accumulate in the suspensory ligament and other tissues. This raises a question: Since hyaluronic acid and chondroitin sulfate are both proteoglycans, would supplementing them cause further damage to a horse with DSLD? I have found no studies on this, but if proteoglycans are already accumulating because of a genetic disorder, it would make some sense not to supplement them.

In fact, when you're dealing with a problem such as DSLD or any kind of ligament injury for that matter, joint supplementation is really not the way to go. For ligament health and repair, there are five things that I pay attention to, in addition to a healthy diet:

- Vitamin E, at least 5000 IU per day for a full-sized horse, even upwards of 8000 units a day depending on the severity of the problem.
- Vitamin B6 as part of a B complex–and you can add extra, up to a maximum of 200 mg a day.
- Omega-3 fatty acids—ground flaxseed, chia seeds, or the omega preparation, Omega-3F (Kauffman) that I mentioned previously. Omega 3s are very important.
- MSM is an anti-inflammatory; give at least 10,000 mg a day.
- CoQ10, for which you will probably have to buy the human version at your local drug store or online. Give between 50 and 100 mg per 100 pounds of body weight. Note: You don't have to pierce the capsules if you feed them with something that you moisten; you can throw it in the feed and the horse will generally eat it.

DSLD and insulin resistance. Lynn also asks if there is any supplement that can be fed to a horse with DSLD that is also appropriate for a horse that is insulin resistant.

Answer. Since the DSLD horse won't need a joint supplement, we're not concerned about any glucosamine that increases insulin. In general, follow the recommended diet for any insulin resistant horse: Stay away from sugars and starches. Stay away from oats, corn, barley, anything made with sweetening like molasses. Stay away from carrots and apples, those types of things. Ground flaxseed with its omega 3s is excellent for an insulin-resistant horse.

AniFlex Complete (AniMed). Theresa asks about this supplement.

Answer. It has a very small amount of vitamin E, only 55 IUs, which is frankly negligible. It contains a small amount of glucosamine and some bioflavonoids. It has a very small amount of MSM. It has only 50 mg of HA. It has very little omega 3s. It has selenium in it, which is only 0.5 mg in one serving; however, you have to look at other sources of selenium to avoid a toxic overdose—it is best not to have more than 3 mg of selenium in the total diet. Better, more effective choices would be the Matrix 5-H/A, the HylaSport or the Actiflex.

Equi-Bone (TLC Animal Nutrition). Cindy S. has a horse that has a fracture of the navicular. She wants my opinion on this product.

Answer. First, look at the horse's whole diet to determine his overall vitamin and mineral needs, then determine whether the ingredients in this product fill in the gaps properly. Equi-bone has a lot of vitamins and minerals, so you should guard against overdoing those. For bone repair itself, the key ingredient is silica; it is a very, very important component of bone. In addition, feed quality protein and vitamin B6 for protein production. For silica, I recommend OrthoPur Si made by HorseTech.

From my book, Feed Your Horse Like a Horse, here's the full list of "Nutrients to Heal a Broken Bone"—remember, these are therapeutic levels.

- Soybean meal or protein supplement — 200 g protein per 100 lbs of body weight
- Vitamin C — 20 mg per pound of body weight
- Vitamin B6 — 0.15 mg per pound of body weight
- Silica (orthosilicic acid) — 0.4 mg per pound of body weight
- Vitamin A — 50 IU per pound of body weight
- Vitamin E — 5 IU per pound of body weight
- Alfalfa — 2:1 grass to alfalfa for calcium and phosphorus
- Magnesium — 5,000 mg per 500 lbs of body weight
- Copper — 12 mg per 100 lbs of body weight
- Zinc and manganese — 48 mg per 100 lbs body weight
- Hyaluronic acid — 10 mg per 100 lbs of body weight

Spotlight on Equine Nutrition Series

GLC 5500 (GLCDirect). Cindy also asks about this product.

Answer. This contains a proprietary product called Actistatin Equine, which the manufacturer claims significantly increases glucosamine and chondroitin sulfate. GLC has posted a study online that looks very impressive. However, about this and any claims for a proprietary product: First, I have no idea what Actistatin (or any proprietary product) is; it may be very nice, but without knowing its makeup, I don't know if it is truly beneficial or whether there are long-term effects from its use; and second, the study was done by a private lab contracted by the company—it wasn't done as a comparison study to another product such as a generic glucosamine and chondroitin sulfate, which raises questions about scientific validity.

Kelp. Cindy wants to know if kelp has healing properties.

Answer. About kelp, be careful. Make sure the product packaging gives you the guaranteed analysis. I'm always concerned about too much iodine in kelp—some is fine, but some kelp products have too much. What you're really after is salt, which is the main ingredient in kelp. Kelp has trace minerals and it may have selenium, so there is an element of risk for the balanced diet unless you know exactly what's in it. Healing properties? Not really, except that salt is very important to the horse's allover health, for a variety of reasons.

Cetyl M (myristoleate) for injury. Eileen has a 25-year-old quarter horse mare whose spine and tail are completely out of alignment due to an injury following an altercation with another horse. Eileen asks if the continued use of cetyl M will help alleviate the mare's back and hock pain, and if there is a better alternative. Eileen uses bute only when she has to.

Answer. Cetyl M is a fine supplement, but Cetyl-Flex H/A has more of the myristoleate and so is more potent. With either product, be sure to add vitamin C because of your horse's age. Add some ground flaxseed or you might even go with Kauffman's Omega-3F which contains the fish oils. Make sure the diet has enough B vitamins and quality protein as well. If the cetyl M or Cetyl-Flex H/A is not helping, try the KeraFlex EQ and see if that helps. (See also Appendix B, for information about the anti-inflammatory properties of curcumin.)

Regarding the bute, remember it carries a significant ulcer risk. Instead, try a good bute-less preparation. One that I like that's very concentrated is called SU-PER suBstitUTE (Gateway). It does have devil's claw in it, which should never be given to a pregnant mare.

H/A gel vs powder. Valletta uses a product called Lubrisyn (Lubrisyn) and asks if there's any difference in the absorption of the gel form as opposed to the powder.

Answer. There is not a significant difference. The gel has more water and anything that's fluid is likely to be better absorbed initially, but frankly the powder gets mixed with water anyway when it hits the digestive tract so there really isn't a significant difference in that regard. I would go with what's easier to feed.

Clarifications on feeding flaxseed. Joyce asks for clarification: is the recommendation a half-cup of flaxseed per 400 pounds of horse?

Answer. That's a half cup of *ground* flaxseed; you never want to feed whole flax seeds. Remember that ground flaxseed starts to go rancid almost immediately, so you must feed it right away. Do not store it to use tomorrow or the next day. Also, flax seeds have about three times more phosphorus than calcium, which is upside down from the desirable ratio. If the diet has calcium from other sources, then it's not a concern. If you're feeding some alfalfa, for example, or if your hay has adequate calcium, then it's certainly not an issue. But if you're feeding something else that also has too much phosphorus (bran, for example), you need to exercise caution. That's why I often recommend a prepared product like Nutra-Flax (HorseTech) that is stabilized so you don't have to grind it every day. It has about a one year shelf life and it also has calcium added to correct for that naturally inverted ratio.

It's important to note that ½ cup is 4 fluid ounces, but when filled with ground flaxseed, it weighs 2 ounces (56.75 grams).

Polyglycan as preventive. Barbara asks about a product called Polyglycan (Arthrodynamic Laboratories). Her veterinarian recommended that she give this to her horse about every six weeks as a preventive. The horse is 20, and her joint x-rays show no arthritis.

Answer. The first approach with older horses that are not having any symptoms certainly is the vitamin C and flaxseed route. Do that first and then three or four months down the road see how she's doing. You can always consider doing the injections. Polyglycan contains hyaluronic acid, chondroitin sulfate, and glucosamine. Keep in mind that glucosamine may not be appropriate for insulin resistant horses, and injections carry risks.

Platinum Performance. Cindy L. has a 20-year-old cushingoid, insulin-resistant horse on Platinum Performance; she wonders if this is adequate.

Answer. Platinum Performance is a good supplement in general. BUT for the insulin-resistant horse, there are a couple of things that concern me. Number one, it contains iron. Although it doesn't have much, I really like to avoid iron if I can. My second concern is that it does contain some molasses—again, not a lot, but I have reservations about giving any molasses to an insulin resistant horse.

Also, Platinum Performance offers only 740 IU of vitamin E, and no vitamin C (necessary for the older horse). I prefer the Glanzen Complete, which is like Platinum Performance in that it's flax based, but it does not contain iron or any molasses, and it has a full complement of minerals and vitamins, including 2500 IUs of vitamin E and 2500 mg of vitamin C.

For the 20 year old horse, I would add Flex IR to the Glanzen Complete as a joint support and another 1500 mg of vitamin C, bringing the total to 4000 mg. C-442 (HorseTech) is a buffered vitamin C which is a nice product. Pure C (Vita Flex) is also worthwhile. Ester C (Med Vet) is appropriate for horses prone toward ulcers.

Legend and ulcers. Jamie has a horse that was recently diagnosed with ulcers in his large intestine; he is now on an ulcer medication. He's 16 years old, a thoroughbred, and a former racetrack horse. Jamie took ownership of him a short time ago. He's sound, but has some arthritis in his knees and one of his fetlocks. His previous owner had him on Legend IV shots every quarter for the past three years. But since she has the ulcer issue with him now (and he had a recent episode of colic), she wants to be careful about what she gives him. She thinks his diet should be evaluated.

Answer. Legend shots present no risk for his digestive tract, and if the product is working, then stay with it. As far as the ulcer is concerned, that requires some special care; it's kind of a little off topic and so I suggest that you listen to my teleseminar specifically addressing ulcers and read my article on lecithin on my website[ii]. In general, though, feed your horse forage free-choice (see Appendix A), then add to that a good vitamin/mineral supplement. Omega 3s from ground flaxseed will reduce inflammation and then there's a very nice herbal preparation that I like a lot for ulcers called Amiquell (HorseTech). I also recommend Starting Gate Nutritional Granules (SBS Equine) with lecithin and apple pectin.

Let me conclude with this reminder: Take a look first at the basics. Start with a good nutritional foundation—often improving that will be all you need to assure your horse's joint health. But then, if you need to go further, build on that with various supplements and treatments. Remember this can often be a trial and error process, so don't let it frustrate you. There are many options to choose from.

---

[i] Many products mentioned in this book are available through my online store at www.gettyequinenutrition.com.

[ii] See Dr. Juliet M. Getty's article, "Lecithin Inhibits Bute-related Ulcers", at www.gettyequinenutrition.com, in the Library section.

Appendix A
What It Means to Feed Free Choice

The horse's digestive tract is designed to have forage flowing through it every minute of every day. At night, too!

The intestines are made of muscles and require forage to keep them exercised and conditioned, in order to assure efficient nutrient processing and prevent colic. Furthermore, the horse's stomach continuously secretes acid, even when empty; horses need to chew to produce saliva, a natural antacid. Running out of hay is physically painful and mentally stressful, virtually assuring the formation of an ulcer. But that's not all – the hormonal response created by forage restriction tells the horse to hold on to body fat, creating a weight management nightmare and making it very difficult for the overweight horse to lose weight.

The solution: Feed your horse the way he was designed to eat.

Step 1: *Know what you are feeding.* Test your hay and/or pasture. Especially when feeding overweight horses, the forage should be low in non-structural carbohydrates (NSC)—NSC should be less than 12% on an as-sampled basis. And it should be low in calories (known as digestible energy) at no more than 0.88 Mcals/lb on an as-sampled basis.

Step 2: Once you have determined the forage is appropriate to feed, **feed it free choice**. Always have forage available, 24/7. The hay should never run out, not even for 10 minutes. And not just during the day—nighttime is important, too.

Then be patient, step back and watch your horse do what comes naturally. Give the process approximately 2-3 weeks; most horses take less time, some take up to a month. At first he will overeat, but once he understands that the hay is always there, he will walk away – that's the magic moment! He will calm down, eat more slowly, and self-regulate his intake, eating only what his body needs to maintain condition.

Allow your horse to tell you how much he needs. He may even eat less than before because running out of hay is no longer an issue. Trust this will happen. Soon, your horse's weight will adjust into the normal, healthy range, his behavior will be more natural and steady, and his health will be more vibrant.

Appendix B
Consider Curcumin for Joint Inflammation
by Juliet M. Getty, Ph.D.

Author's note: This article was written after the teleseminar and offers updated information on counteracting inflammation.

Ever hear of curcumin? It's the active ingredient in the spice, turmeric, which has been used for centuries in Indian cooking, as well as in Ayurvedic medicine. It exhibits anti-oxidant properties (neutralizing damaging free radicals), and has been used to treat a long list of conditions, including diarrhea, respiratory infections, dermatitis, and even cancerous tumors.

Most notably, curcumin reduces inflammation and pain by inhibiting the cyclooxygenase enzyme 2 (COX-2), while maintaining COX-1 enzymatic function. That's good news, because the COX-1 enzyme protects your horse's stomach lining. COX-2 inhibition is a far better route to take for pain control than the more commonly used non-steroidal anti-inflammatory drugs (NSAIDs) such as phenylbutazone (bute), flunixin meglumin (Banamine), or aspirin; these inhibit not only COX-2 enzymes, but also the protective COX-1 enzymes. Firocoxib (known as Equioxx for horses and Previcox for dogs) is an NSAID that only inhibits the COX-2 enzyme, offering a safer option for horse owners. But curcumin supplementation offers a natural approach that can be highly effective and far less costly.

Osteoarthritis is a common source of pain for horses. This disease is characterized by a progressive deterioration of joint cartilage, making it less able to protect the joint against friction. The underlying cause of pain is due to a release of cytokines and reactive oxygen species -- inflammatory substances that can lead to further degradation of joint tissue. There are many joint supplements on the market designed to slow down cartilage loss, increase production of lubricating synovial fluid, and reduce pain. Curcumin is not typically added to these joint supplement preparations. Furthermore, it can be a natural alternative to intra-articular hyaluronic acid or polysulfated glycosaminoglycan (PGAG) injections.

What is Turmeric/Curcumin?

Turmeric is derived from the underground stems (rhizomes) of the plant *Curcuma longa*, a member of the ginger family. It has the familiar yellow color of Indian curry and American mustard. Curcumin is the biologically active phytochemical found in turmeric. Chemically known as diferuloylmethane, with a molecular formula $C_{21}H_{20}O_6$, it has been shown to have dramatic health benefits. Most research involving curcumin has been done with humans. However, researchers[1] from the United Kingdom and Germany recently revealed that curcumin significantly reduces the inflammatory pathways found in horses suffering from osteoarthritis. Thomas Schell, DVM (developer of Cur-Ost), has also done extensive research[2] on the use of curcumin's therapeutic action on equine osteoarthritis. Using Quarter Horses, Morgans, Thoroughbreds, Arabians, and Paso Finos, all with varying degrees of lameness from degenerative arthritis, he found improvement when comparing lameness scores before and after administration of a nutritional formula containing curcumin, as well as vitamins E and C.

Safety and Dosage

With humans, dosages as high as 12 grams per day[3] for a three month period have been shown to be safe. For longer term supplementation, 500 mgs per day is more readily accepted. This equals ¼ teaspoon of turmeric.

An appropriate dosage for horses has not been established, though one tablespoon per day works well as a maintenance dose. If diarrhea or changes in appetite occur, discontinue use. Do not administer NSAIDS along with turmeric or curcumin-containing compounds. Also keep in mind that turmeric slows blood clotting and therefore should be discontinued if you are planning any surgical procedures.

Personal experience

My off-the-track Thoroughbred suffers from osteochondral fragments (bone chips) in his fetlock joint. Originally I treated him with a low dose of bute, along with lecithin[4] to prevent gastric ulcers, but I switched to feeding turmeric at a dosage of two tablespoons per day. I kept feeding lecithin as a precaution. He is doing just as well as he did with bute, and his limping has not returned. He runs in the pasture with ease. After two months on this two-tablespoon therapeutic dose, I have decreased it to one tablespoon per day and will soon reduce it further, relying on more only as needed. I have found it to be palatable and easy to mix with feeds.

Summary

Take a look at what curcumin has to offer. Turmeric is easy to get in bulk at whole food stores or on line. It may just be the extra ingredient your horse needs to be comfortable and pain-free.

---

[1] Clutterbuck, A.L., Mobasheri, A., Shakibaei, M., Allaway, D., and Harris, P., 2009. Interleukin-1B-Induced extracellular matrix degradation and glycosaminoglycan release is inhibited by curcumin in an explant model of cartilage inflammation. *Annals of the New York Academy of Sciences*, 1171, 428-435.

[2] Schell, T. 2009. A promising natural therapy for equine osteoarthritis. *Journal of the American Holistic Medical Association*, 28(1), 11-15.

[3] Goel, A., Kunnumakkara, A.B., & Aggarwal, B.B. 2008. Curcumin as "Curecumin": from kitchen to clinic. *Biochemical Pharmacology*, 75(4), 787-809.

[4] Getty, J.M. 2013. Lecithin inhibits bute-related ulcers. Getty Equine Nutrition, LLC. www.gettyequinenutrition.com.

Made in the USA
Charleston, SC
07 April 2015